THE WINDMILL

David and Andrew enjoye
farm in the wild and lone
the nearby caves and spen
house attic.

But once the windmill was bu   ⌐ ⌐ʜanged — and
not for the better.

Gary Crew and Steven Woolman, winners of the Childrens'
Book Council of Australia's Picture Book of the Year
award for *The Watertower*, will hold readers in suspense
with this gripping science fiction tale.

Published by Era Publications,
220 Grange Road, Flinders Park, SA 5025 Australia

Text © Gary Crew, 1998
Illustrations © Era Publications, 1998
Illustration by Steven Woolman
Printed in Hong Kong
First published 1998

**National Library of Australia
Cataloguing-in-Publication Data:**
Crew, Gary, 1947-
     The windmill.

     ISBN 1 86374 430 4.

     I. Woolman, Steven. II. Title.

A823.3

For worldwide distribution details of
this book see Era Publications' web site:
http://www.era-publications.com.au

15   14   13   12   11   10   9   8   7   6   5   4   3   2   1

The Windmill

Written by Gary Crew
Illustrated by Steven Woolman

JUNIOR
NOVELS

CHAPTER 1

There had been a time when the Dalton boys had liked taking holidays at Old Rusty's farm, but once the windmill was built, something changed — and not for the better.

Old Rusty had been a friend of the boys' Grandad since the war. He'd never married or had children of his own. Grandad used to say that all the fighting and bloodshed had 'knocked Old Rusty around something terrible'. It wasn't too hard to see how. Even though he ran the farm on his own, Rusty had only one leg. The other had been sliced off by shrapnel. Still, he kept to himself and never seemed to have any trouble getting about the place, rough and tumble as it was.

Rusty owned a goat farm in a wild and lonely valley full of limestone caves and landslips and thick wooded forests, but he managed well enough. "He handles a crutch like a second leg," the boys' Grandad used to say.

The boys knew that this was true. More than once they'd seen Rusty's bright red hair disappear over a ledge before they had even reached the side. Next minute he'd bob up holding a lost goat and saying, "Heck, what's the matter with boys today? Why when I was a lad . . ." and then off he'd go telling one of his stories about life on the farm 'in the good old days' before 'technology came'.

'Technology' to Old Rusty meant just about anything invented after the radio. He certainly didn't have a TV, and the boys, David and Andrew, used to wonder if he'd even heard of a CD player — but that's why they had always liked the farm.

It was fun to climb the rickety ladders in the weathered barn, or crawl around with candles in the limestone caves, dodging stalagmites and stalactites, watching the changing shadows cast on the slimy, dripping walls and imagining what horrible creatures they might be.

Best of all they liked spending their nights in the farmhouse attic.

When Old Rusty had cleared away the dinner dishes (he always served up sausages with tomato sauce and lashings of mashed potato and big fat juicy peas) there was nothing to do but go to bed — unless, of course, the boys stayed down in the parlour with Rusty and listened to his ancient console radio.

Rusty was a bit of a classical music fan. The farmhouse had an enormous ham radio aerial made of junk steel and wire mounted on the roof. He used the aerial to pick up concerts from all over the world.

The boys weren't into classical music. They would rather scramble up the narrow attic stairs with a kerosene lamp each and read their books, just listening to the music drift softly up from below. There was a nice cosy feeling about being lulled to sleep like that.

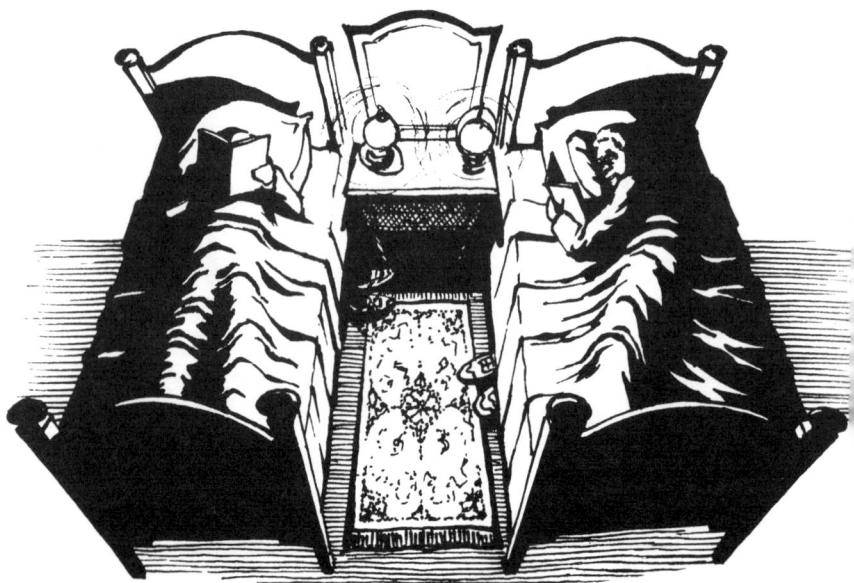

Until the windmill was built, that is.

David and Andrew remembered how upset Rusty had been when the first notification had come from the Public Energy Board.

"What's a windmill got to do with energy?" he wanted to know.

"Rusty, it's not a windmill for drawing water, or grinding corn," Andrew explained. "It's a new method of generating power. You know, for electricity. You wouldn't have your radio if you didn't have electricity."

Sometimes the boys were embarrassed talking like this to Rusty. It made them sound as if they were talking down to him — as if he lived in the Dark Ages and didn't know anything.

"Well, if it's more electricity they want to generate for all their new-fangled machines, there's plenty of coal in this county. What's wrong with using that? It was good enough when I was a boy — before all this new-fangled technology came along."

David tried to clarify matters. "But Rusty, coal's a fossil fuel. Sooner or later it will all be used up. Burning coal in a power station is a very dirty way of producing energy. It's not good for the ozone layer."

"And there's a nuclear power station at Anglesea, not far from here," Andrew chimed in. "You never read too much about it, but there are rumours that they've had the odd problem out there — the odd 'Red Alert' as they say. The last thing the world wants is a nuclear meltdown. Look what happened at Chernobyl."

"What the hell's a 'chernobyl'?"

"Chernobyl's not a thing, Rusty. It's a place in Russia. There was a terrible nuclear power plant disaster there. Children are still being born with deformities. There could even be mutations."

"Humph," Rusty grunted. "All I know about the Russians is that they write great music — or they did once."

"Rusty," David cut in. "The windmill they're talking about building is a cheap and clean method of producing power. You can never use up all the wind in the world and we'd get to have cleaner air."

But Rusty wasn't listening. It was clear to the boys that they were never going to convince him that any new form of technology was any good. "Anyway," he'd say, "this windmill business is only going to bring trouble. Just you wait and see."

CHAPTER 2

As it turned out, nothing Old Rusty had to say could put a stop to progress, and the construction of the windmill went ahead.

The next time the boys visited the farm they saw that the concrete foundations had been poured, and soon after that, the stainless steel pillar that was to support the sails was hoisted into place.

"It's huge," Andrew said, over-awed by the sight. "It dominates the whole of Rusty's farm."

What he said was true. The windmill was being built on a hill not a hundred metres from the house, right above the honeycomb of caves far below.

"We had better get down and take a look at those caves," David announced ruefully at breakfast one morning. "The way that construction's going they will be ruined soon."

"Yeah," Andrew agreed, slurping a spoonful of Rusty's famous porridge. "The rotten part is that those stalagmites and stalactites have taken about a million years to form — and they're still growing — but the workers out there could destroy them in a couple of days."

"Yeah," said David. "And what for? An ugly steel pipe and some concrete foundations."

That morning the boys took candles and made their way up the hill to the cave entrance. As usual the place had a musty atmosphere that was heightened by the ooze seeping from the walls.

"Yuck," Andrew muttered. "I hate touching that slimy stuff — and it feels slimier than ever. What do you reckon it is?"

Through the darkness in front of him, he could just make out his brother shaking his head. "Geez you're a worry sometimes Andy," David said. "It's seepage from the hill above us. What did you think it was? Nuclear waste?"

Andrew didn't answer. Like all younger brothers he was used to being put down. But he could wait for his revenge. He could . . .

"Look out!" Suddenly his thoughts were interrupted by David's warning shout. "We were right," David explained, holding his candle high to reveal a floor to ceiling column of sandstone that had snapped in two. "This break is recent. See? It's so new that there's not even any slimy stuff growing on the surface. I bet the blasting and digging for the windmill foundations has caused that."

"Oh yeah?" Andrew sneered, now holding his own candle higher to better light the walls. "So, David Dalton, PI, Sleuth of the Ages, Master of Detection . . . How do you account for these marks then?" As he spoke he pointed to a pattern of deep and regular incisions on the wall.

"These look fresh too, but I don't reckon any construction worker came all the way down here to make them with his screwdriver. As a matter of fact, I reckon they look a bit like scratches made by an animal. What do you say to that, oh All Wise Geologist — or should that be Zoologist — of the Universe?" Andrew was very pleased with his find. He couldn't believe that he'd been able to get his own back on David so soon.

Still, big brothers are often hard to convince: "You think I'm that easily fooled? I bet you just made those with your penknife. Trying to get one up on me, eh?"

But as David lunged at his brother to give him a good-natured shove, from out of the darkness there came a peculiar high-pitched sound, like a wire or a cable under stress, and then a long, deep rumble, like something huge being moved — perhaps a boulder or slab of sandstone — and immediately the boys forgot their petty rivalry and ran.

They burst into the sunlight and caught their breath. No extra cables had been hoisted that might have made the high-pitched whining, and no extra concrete foundations had been poured that might have made the grinding sound. In fact, nothing on the construction site had changed at all — except that three metal sails had been attached to the windmill pillar.

And what stunning sails they were.

"They're really something," David gasped. "But why are they called sails when they look so much like wings? Giant silver wings!"

"They do look out of place beside the old farm," Andrew commented, wide-eyed. "Almost . . . almost . . ." but he couldn't think of the right word.

"Alien. That's what they look like," David helped him out.

"As if they're part of some alien technology. No wonder Rusty hates the windmill so much. His farm used to look so cosy and warm, all nestled down into the valley. But now that awful thing just makes it look old fashioned."

"Almost like it's in the way. And the radio aerial on his roof looks even more like junk now."

But the boys had not experienced the worst of 'this new-fangled technology' yet — not by a long shot.

CHAPTER 3

The week the windmill was put into operation was the first of the winter vacation and the boys had gone to stay at the farm. They were looking forward to the same good times they always experienced there, but a lot had changed — and not just the scenery.

Old Rusty seemed moodier for one thing. He moped about the farm muttering to himself about technicians crawling all over his land, sticking their noses in where they weren't wanted. He complained that the goats were going further into the hills or getting lost in the woods in their attempts to get away from all the hustle and bustle. And it was true that some of the better pastures on the low-lands had been badly churned up by construction vehicles.

"You call this progress?" he asked the boys over dinner on their first night. "I call it an invasion. A man goes to fight a war for his country and then, when he's an old codger like me, he expects to find some peace. What's going on here is an invasion of a man's home, that's what it is."

The entire meal was so depressing that the boys actually lost their appetite for sausages and tomato sauce and lashings of mashed potato. "And there aren't any big fat juicy peas because I couldn't be bothered pickin' any," Rusty said gruffly.

After dinner the boys went slowly up to bed. At least that wouldn't have changed they thought, expecting to hear Rusty's sleepy music drifting up to them. But they were in for a rude surprise. Hardly had they trimmed their lamps and climbed into bed, all ready for a good read, when quite a different sound filled the attic.

It was a peculiar high-pitched whirring, not unlike the sound of a cricket in the hearth, but never so pleasant and dreamy. If Rusty was playing his night-time music they certainly couldn't hear it. The whirring attacked their ears. It seemed to penetrate the brain itself. Like torture.

"What's that *noise*?" Andrew demanded of the darkness. "It's terrible."

"Insects?" David offered. "A nest of insects in the rafters?"

They threw back the covers and turned up their lamps and searched high and low but there was no sign of insects, no matter how well camouflaged they might be.

The boys stopped and listened.

"It seems to be coming from outside," David suggested, opening the attic windows.

It was the loveliest night. A full moon hung in the sky like a Chinese lantern and all about the stars winked and twinkled as if to say, "Hey boys, good to see you back."

The boys were no longer certain that they *were* glad to be back. Not only was the whirring sound becoming more irritating every second, but the harsh perpendicular pillar of the windmill seemed to cut Old Rusty's farm clean in half. And those nasty angular sails spinning around and around didn't help much either.

Everything the boys had ever loved about the view now looked so geometric . . . so technical . . . so alien.

Then suddenly they knew. They looked at each other wide-eyed and open-mouthed. They covered their ears and yelled, "It's the windmill. The noise is coming from the windmill!"

Of course this was true.

"So how are we going to get to sleep?" David wanted to know.

"We could get some cotton wool from the medicine cabinet downstairs. We could put that in our ears," Andrew suggested and, since that seemed like the only sensible thing to do, the boys trooped down to get some.

CHAPTER 4

As they reached the parlour they saw Rusty on his knees in front of the old console radio. "Come on now, me darlin'," he was muttering as he tried to tune it in. "Don't let me down after all these years."

The noise coming from the speaker was certainly not classical music. It sounded like static. In fact, it didn't even sound as good as static.

The boys exchanged glances. It was the sound of insects again! But this time it was not a high-pitched whirring. No, it was more of an insect's song with a sort of rising and falling rhythm to it — yet it was coming from the radio.

"What's the trouble Rusty?" Andrew asked as brightly as he could manage. "Problem with an overseas broadcast?"

"Sounds like more than trouble. Sounds like the New York Philharmonic's trying to play 'The Flight of the Bumblebee' under water, eh?"

"Wouldn't just be crossed cables in your aerial, would it?" David was only trying to help but the truth was that he didn't have clue what he was talking about.

To the boys' surprise Rusty agreed. "Might take a look outside and see. Wouldn't be the first time I'd had a stork nesting in the wires."

He opened the door and stepped out into the moonlit yard. The wires of the old aerial were silhouetted against the moon as clear as the pattern of a spider's web on a window.

"Nope, no trouble there."

The words were hardly out of his mouth when a gigantic black shadow swooped down upon them and all three dropped to the ground, gasping.

"Holy moly," Rusty yelled, taking his hands from his head. "That wasn't no stork. Whatever it was, it tried to attack us."

The boys clung together, their faces as pale as ghosts.

"What could it have been? An owl? We've seen plenty in the barn."

"Or a giant bat?"

"I don't know," Rusty admitted, his voice shaking. "I really don't . . ."

Then the creature attacked again. It swooped so low that it couldn't rise in time to clear the roof, and the chimney pot went clattering down the shingles.

"Inside boys." Rusty ordered. "We're being strafed."

CHAPTER 5

Rusty and the boys spent that night huddled on the friendly old Genoa lounge in the parlour.

"Good job I've only got the one leg," the old man joked. "Gives you two scaredy-cats more room to cuddle in, eh? Not that an old trooper like me would be much use in an invasion any more."

Andrew and David said nothing. If they had opened their mouths they might have burst out crying, that's how afraid they were.

Nor was the next night any better.

No sooner had the boys made their way cautiously up the attic stairs, hoping to get a good night's sleep, than the terrible clattering on the shingles directly above them started again. It was so loud that even the eerie whirring of the windmill was drowned out. For a while, at least.

But the boys weren't prepared to lie there and listen. They snuffed their lamps and went stumbling back down the darkened stairs.

There was Old Rusty, trying to tune his buzzing radio again.

"What the hell goes on here?" he moaned. "I've never heard anything like this before. We've got kamikaze bats on the roof — and that damn whirring from the windmill is driving me nuts.

I told you two that this tampering with nature would lead to no good. Unnatural, it is. Unnatural."

"Alien even," Andrew muttered into the darkness.

"Alien . . . " David whispered back.

And in the morning, when the boys saw that a fourth sail had appeared upon the windmill — looking for all the world like the veined and diaphanous wing of an insect — they knew that this was true.